Rosie's Perspective

—— Dog only knows ——

by
Rosie G

Balboa Press books may be ordered through booksellers or by contacting:

Balboa Press
A Division of Hay House
1663 Liberty Drive
Bloomington, IN 47403
www.balboapress.com
1 (877) 407-4847

ISBN: 978-1-5043-4280-3 (sc)
ISBN: 978-1-5043-4281-0 (e)

Print information available on the last page.

Balboa Press rev. date: 1/12/2016

BALBOA
PRESS
A DIVISION OF HAY HOUSE

Who Am I?

My name is Rosie G.

I'm an eleven year old Red Cloud Kelpie from Western Australia.

I understand three languages – Australian, American, and Hawaiian.

I'm clever and can herd humans.

I think about things and look at them from a new perspective.

Let me explain…

Dog loves you

We are loyal, never question,
and love you unconditionally.

Lord Kaplan

Makena

Will of dog

We are patient, persistent
and ALWAYS there for you.

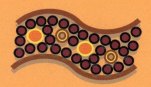

Pua

Word of dog

Buster

We talk to you all the time,
you just have to listen.

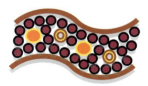

Kachina

Dog's rules

Sometimes we have to be a bossy boots.

Welcome to my boat

I live here....you don't.
If you don't like dog hair on the boat,
stay off.

To you, I'm just a dog...
To me and my parents,
I'm intelligent, fast,
speak my mind,
and love adventure.

My parents say
I'm as good a sailor
as most humans.

Rosie

Doing dog's work

Love what you do.

Pudding & Nimble

Faithful to dog

We are to you.

ClaireBelle

Talking with dog

Dog is wise.

You can learn a lot from dog.

Nimble

Dog's plan

Usually it's good for you.

Honey & Freckles

Honey & Freckles

Plan to swim, jump and play whenever you can.

Pudding , Nimble & Bud

Dog bless you!

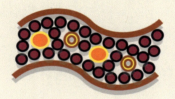

You are our best mate,

we love you.

We even love cats!

Kiki & Baby

Dog is love

Love to play, love to eat,

love to nap, love to be.

Nash

Dog only knows

Nimble

We *know* everything.

For dog's sake

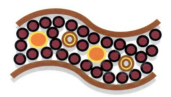

Nimble

Naia

Bud

Jamie Lubin

Be silly once in awhile
and wag your tail.

You'll feel much better!

Dog bless the child

We love children.

They know dog.

CeCe & baby Lucy

Sevin

Honest to dog!

Surfing this HUGE wave…

really he was!

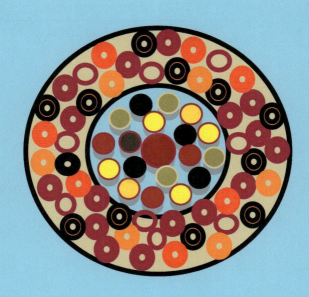

Dogfearing man

Smart human.

Casterton Kelpie Muster

Dogless man

Unhappy human.

LIFE WITHOUT DOGS... I DON'T THINK SO

Good dog!

What a mess!

Oh well.

Pudding & Nimble

Dog awful tired

Time for a well-earned nap.

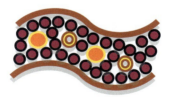

Ronan

Rosie

Dog awful noise!

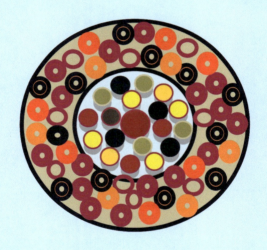

Don't bark so loud!

Rosie

Dog day afternoon

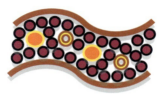

Nimble & Pudding

Nimble

Time for another nap.

Or another...

Nimble

Rosie

Bud & Nimble

Lucy

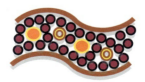

Hooch

Or another....

Or another....

ClaireBelle

Bailey Butt

Cleanliness is next to dogliness

As long as it doesn't mean a BATH!

Rosie

Dog dammit!

Don't say our name in vain.

We love you.

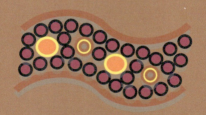

Lucky , Lily & Bozeman

Dog works in mysterious ways

Beloka Kelpie Stud
© WorkingDogRescue.com.a

Rosie

We always have a reason….

Nimble

Child of dog

Yep, smart puppy.

Tricky

Dog is on our side!

Dog is by our side.

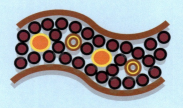

Always.

Rosie & mate

Dog helps those who help themselves

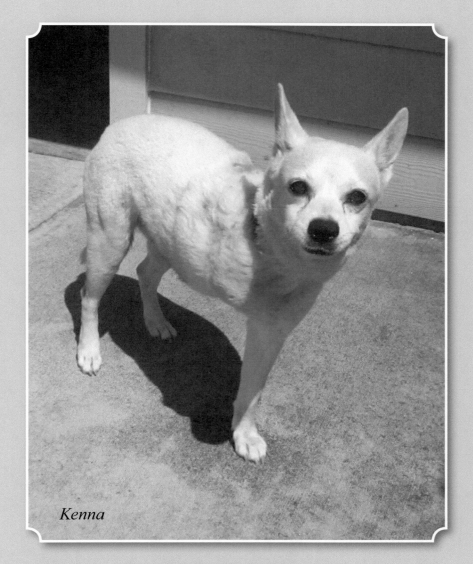

Kenna

Go with what you got.

Dog's little acre

ClaireBelle

ClaireBelle

A place of peace

Dogdamn lucky

Yep we are!

ClaireBelle

There but for the grace of dog I go

Rosie

Henna

We will keep watch for you.

Thank dog for that!

You're welcome.

Honey

Dog is great!

Theo

Yes we are!

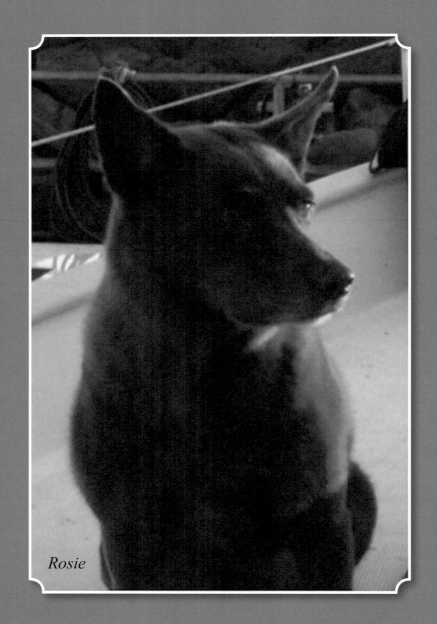

Rosie

Dog-like

Yes you can be.

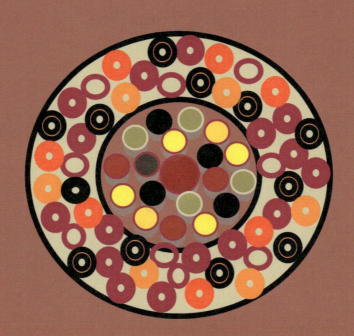

Oh my dog!

Know that dog loves you -

no matter how you are,

where you are,

how you feel,

or what you do,

we are there for you!

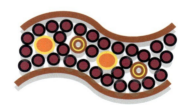

Rosie & mate

In dog we trust

You can.

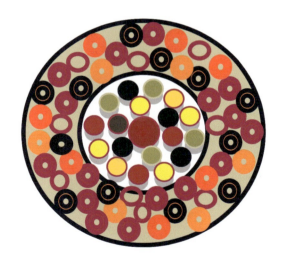

True Love

always has your back

AWDRI WorkingDogRescue.com.au

75

Thank dog for humans!

We can't do it without you!

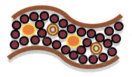 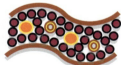 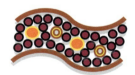

Puppy Poo

Dog only knows

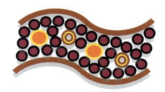

Rosie G

August 2015

Rosie

Thanks to:

Special thanks to all the humans who provided the photos of my mates:-

Baby & Kiki photographed by Richard Kellom

Bailey Butt, CeCe & Lucy photographed by Zeppo Spanier

Bonnie photographed by Rosslyn Ganfield

Bozeman, Lily, Lucky & Pua photographed by Diane Krieger, www.oceandesigns.com

Bud, Chip, Nimble, Pudding & Tricky photographed by Australian Working Dog Rescue, www.workingdogrescue.com.au

Buster photographed by Daniel Southmayd, www.cateringfromsouptonuts.com

ClaireBelle photographed by Kerstin Edwards

Henna & Theo photographed by Sandra Adams

Freckles & Honey photographed by Jennifer Lynn, www.wisdomflowyoga.com

Hooch & Nash photographed by Roy Van Raden

Jamie Lubin & Kachina photographed by Robert Masters, www.bestmedia.com

Kenna & Naia photographed by Larry Pacheco

Lord Kaplan, Makena & Rosie photographed by Samantha Spanier, www.barryspanier.com

Ronan photographed by Naomi DeFriest

Sevin photographed by Ray Masters, www.raymasters.com

Thanks to my mum, Bonnie, for having me.

And for my human mum for taking

such good care of me.

Printed in the United States
By Bookmasters